30 Minute Meals

Hannie P. Scott

ISBN: 151519647X
ISBN-13: 978-1515196471

ACKNOWLEDGMENTS

I am so grateful for those of you who make up the community of readers that I love to write recipe books for! Thank you for your shares, encouraging emails, feedback, and reviews. I appreciate each one more than you guys know.

Cheesy Pasta Skillet

Servings: 4

What you need:

1 lb ground beef

16-oz package refrigerated tortellini

1 can diced tomatoes

1 small can of tomato sauce

2 cups water

1 tbsp garlic powder

1 tbsp onion powder

2 cups shredded cheddar cheese

What to do:

1. Brown the hamburger meat in a large skillet then drain off the fat.
2. Add the tortellini, water, garlic powder, and onion powder and stir together.
3. Bring the skillet to a boil, reduce heat, and cover.
4. Cook until the tortellini is soft then drain off the excess water.
5. Stir in the diced tomatoes and tomato sauce.
6. Sprinkle the cheese over the mixture evenly and let it melt then serve.

**Serve with Roasted Asparagus.

Goldie Chicken

Servings: 4

What you need:

2 tbsp olive oil

4 chicken breasts

Salt and pepper, to taste

8 cloves garlic

1/2 cup water

1/2 cup brown sugar

1/4 cup rice vinegar

1/2 inch slice of ginger

1 cup chicken broth

1/4 cup soy sauce

Cooked rice

2 scallions or green onions, thinly sliced

What to do:

1. Heat the olive oil in a large skillet over medium high heat.
2. Season the chicken breasts with salt and pepper and cook until golden on the outside and completely white on the inside. Transfer to a plate and set aside.
3. In the same skillet, sauté the cloves of garlic for 2 minutes then put them on the plate with the chicken.
4. Once again, in the same skillet over medium high heat, pour 1/2 cup of water and scrape the bottom of the skillet with a wooden spatula to get all the browned bits dissolved (this is called deglazing the pan).
5. Whisk the brown sugar into the skillet until it is dissolved. Cook for about 5 minutes.
6. Add in the vinegar and stir.

2

7. Add in the garlic, ginger, chicken broth, and soy sauce. Bring to a boil, stirring occasionally. Cook until the sauce thickens, about 10 minutes.

8. Once the sauce has thickened, return the chicken to the skillet and heat.

9. Serve with rice and garnish with scallions or green onions.

**Serve with Sriracha Zucchini.

Hamburger Steaks

Servings: 4

What you need:
1 1/2 lbs ground beef
1/4 cup seasoned bread crumbs
2 tsp Worcestershire sauce
1 onion, thinly sliced
2 tbsp olive oil
1 tbsp butter
2 cups beef broth
1 tbsp cornstarch

What to do:
1. In a large mixing bowl, combine the ground beef, bread crumbs, and 1 tsp of Worcestershire sauce. Divide the mixture into 4 patties.
2. In a large skillet, heat 2 tbsp of olive oil and 1 tbsp of butter over medium-high heat.
3. Add the patties to the skillet and cook on each side until cooked all the way through.
4. Place the patties on a plate and set aside.
5. Add the sliced onions to the same skillet over medium-high heat and cook for 5 minutes.
6. Add the broth, the other tsp of Worcestershire, salt, and pepper to the skillet.
7. In a small bowl, whisk together the cornstarch and 1 tbsp of water. Whisk this mixture into the skillet. Bring to a boil then reduce heat to low.
8. Add the patties back to the skillet and heat through.

Philly Cheesesteak

Servings: 4

What you need:

4 hoagie rolls

2 lbs top sirloin steak, thinly sliced

Salt and pepper, to taste

1 white onion, thinly sliced

1 bell pepper, thinly sliced

1 tsp minced garlic

8 slices provolone cheese

What to do:

1. Preheat your oven to 400 degrees F.
2. Spray a large skillet with cooking spray and heat to medium-high.
3. Season the sliced steak with salt and pepper and cook until cooked through.
4. Add in the onions and peppers and cook until the onions are translucent.
5. Add the garlic and cook for another minute.
6. Slice the hoagie rolls long ways down the center.
7. Place 2 slices of cheese on one side of each roll.
8. Top the other side of each roll with steak, peppers, and onions.
9. Place the open rolls in the oven for 3-5 minutes or until the cheese is melted.

Spicy Shrimp Pasta

Servings: 4

What you need:

1/2 cup olive oil

3 tsp minced garlic

2 tbsp brown sugar

2 tsp soy sauce

2 lbs deveined, peeled shrimp

1/2 tsp red pepper flakes

1/2 cup grated parmesan cheese

8 oz penne noodles

What to do:

1. Cook the noodles according to package directions.
2. Pour the olive oil, garlic, soy sauce, and brown sugar into a large ziplock bag and add in the shrimp.
3. Seal the bag and shake to coat the shrimp with the sauce.
4. Add the shrimp to a large skillet over medium-high heat. Sauté for 3-5 minutes.
5. Add the red pepper flakes, parmesan cheese, and cooked noodles.
6. Cook for another 3-4 minutes until the noodles and shrimp are combined with the cheese.

Double Decker Tacos

Servings: 4

What you need:
1 lb ground beef
1 packet taco seasoning
1/4 cup water
1 can rotel tomatoes
1 15-oz can red kidney beans, drained and rinsed (optional)
8 hard taco shells
8 soft taco shells
1 15-oz can refried beans
Toppings of your choice

What to do:
1. In a large skillet over medium high heat, brown your ground beef then drain off the fat.
2. Stir the water and the taco seasoning into the meat and mix well. Cook for 5 minutes.
3. Add the rotel tomatoes and kidney beans to the meat, if using.
4. Heat the hard taco shells in the oven for 5 minutes at 350 degrees.
5. Heat the soft taco shells in the microwave in for 30 seconds.
6. Heat the refried beans in the microwave or in a saucepan on the stove.
7. Spoon a spoonful of refried beans onto each soft shell and spread evenly.
8. Place the hard taco shell upright down the center of the soft taco shell and stick the soft shell to the hard shell.

9. Spoon ground beef mixture into the hard shell and top with desired toppings. I use onions, lettuce, cheese, and hot sauce.

Simple Shrimp Gumbo

Serves: 4-6

What you need:
1/2 cup vegetable oil
1/2 cup flour
1 quart chicken broth
2 stalks celery, diced
1 bell pepper, diced
1 yellow onion, diced
1 14-oz can whole tomatoes
1 tbsp salt
1/2 tsp black pepper
1 tsp thyme
3 bay leaves
2 tsp Cajun seasoning
1/2 tsp liquid smoke
1 lb cleaned and deveined frozen uncooked shrimp with tails removed

What to do:
1. Heat the vegetable oil in a large skillet over medium-high heat.
2. Sprinkle the flour into the skillet and stir it constantly until the flour has browned. Turn off the heat.
3. Transfer the oil and flour (the roux) to a large soup pot.
4. Pour the chicken broth into the soup pot and bring it to a boil. Lower heat and stir well.
5. Add in the celery, bell pepper, onion, tomatoes, salt, pepper, thyme, bay leaves, and Cajun seasoning.

6. Let everything simmer for 15 minutes, stirring occasionally.
7. Add in the liquid smoke and shrimp and cook for 3-5 minutes, or until shrimp begins to turn pink.
8. Serve over rice.

Corn Soup

Serves: 2-4

What you need:

1 tbsp vegetable oil

1 yellow onion, chopped

2 cups chicken broth

2 ears of corn

1 can creamed corn

1/8 tsp cumin

1/2 tsp salt

1 green onion, finely chopped

Salt and pepper, to taste

3/4 cup plain Greek yogurt

What to do:

1. Cut the corn from the cob and set corn aside.
2. Heat the oil in a soup pot over medium heat and sauté the onion for 3-4 minutes.
3. Add the chicken stock and bring it to a boil then reduce the heat to a simmer.
4. Add the corn, creamed corn, cumin, and salt. Simmer for 15 minutes.
5. Stir in the green onion and plain Greek yogurt. Stir well and simmer for 10 minutes.
6. Season with salt and pepper before serving.

Chicken Tortilla Soup

Serves: 4-6

What you need:

1 tbsp olive oil

2 garlic cloves, minced

4 chicken breasts, chopped into small pieces

2 cans petite diced tomatoes

1 can rotel tomatoes

1 cup salsa

1 tsp ground cumin

1 quart chicken broth

1 cup fresh cilantro, chopped

Salt and pepper, to taste

What to do:

1. Heat olive oil in a large soup pot over medium-high heat.
2. Add the garlic into the pot and sauté for a couple of minutes.
3. Add the chicken pieces to the pot and cook until completely done.
4. Add the diced tomatoes, rotel tomatoes, salsa, and ground cumin. Let simmer for 5 minutes.
5. Add in the chicken broth and let simmer for 20 minutes.
6. Before serving stir in the cilantro, salt, and pepper.

Pepperoni Roll-Ups

Servings: 8

What you need:

1 can crescent rolls

40 slices of pepperoni

4 pieces of mozzarella string cheese, cut in half

Garlic powder

Marinara sauce

What to do:

1. Preheat your oven to 375 degrees F.
2. Unroll the crescent rolls and separate them into 8 triangles.
3. Place 5 pepperonis and one string cheese half on the large end of the crescent roll.
4. Roll up the crescent rolls and sprinkle each of them with garlic powder.
5. Place the rolls on a greased baking sheet and bake for 12-15 minutes, or until golden brown.
6. Serve with warm marinara sauce.

Asian Meatballs

Servings: 10

What you need:

2 lbs ground beef

2 tsp sesame oil

1 cup panko crumbs

½ tsp ground ginger

2 eggs

3 tsp minced garlic

½ cup chopped green onions

Toasted sesame seeds

2/3 cup hoisin sauce

¼ cup rice vinegar

2 cloves garlic, minced

2 tbsp soy sauce

1 tsp sesame oil

1 tsp ground ginger

What to do:

1. Preheat your oven to 400 degrees F.
2. Grease a large baking sheet.
3. In a large bowl, mix together the ground beef, sesame oil. Panko crumbs, ½ tsp ground ginger, 2 eggs, 3 tsp minced garlic, and green onions.
4. Shape this mixture into 1-2 inch balls, the size depending on your preference.
5. Place the balls on the prepared baking sheet.
6. Bake for 12 minutes or until no longer pink on the inside.

7. While the meatballs are baking, mix together the hoisin sauce, rice vinegar, garlic, soy sauce, sesame oil, and ground ginger.

8. When the meatballs are finished baking, dip each one in the sauce and place on a serving dish.

9. Sprinkle toasted sesame seeds over the meatballs.

Mexican Skillet Casserole

Servings: 4

What you need:

2 tsp vegetable oil

1 onion, chopped

4 tsp minced garlic

1 lb ground beef

2 tbsp chili powder

1 tsp ground cumin

1 tsp salt

1 cup long-grain rice

1 tsp salt

1 can rotel tomatoes

1 can black beans, rinsed and drained

2 oz shredded cheddar cheese

What to do:

1. Place 2 cups of water in a small pot. Add the rice and 1 tsp of salt. Bring to a boil. Boil for 7-8 minutes or until rice is done. Drain and set aside.

2. Heat a large skillet over medium-high heat. Add 2 tsp of oil. Saute the onion and garlic for 3 minutes.

3. Brown the ground beef in the same skillet. Drain and return to the skillet.

4. Stir in the chili powder, cumin, and 1 tsp of salt.

5. Add in the cooked rice, rotel tomatoes, and beans. Cook for 2 minutes over medium-high heat.

6. Sprinkle the cheese over the mixture and let stand until the cheese melts.

Chicken Nuggets

Servings: 4

What you need:
1 lb chicken breasts
1/4 cup old fashioned oats
1/4 tsp dried parsley
1/2 tsp garlic powder
1/4 tsp onion powder
1/2 tsp salt
1 cup panko bread crumbs
1 tbsp grated parmesan cheese

What to do:
1. Cut your chicken breasts into chicken nugget sized chunks.
2. Preheat your oven to 375 degrees F.
3. Place the oats, parsley, garlic powder, onion powder, salt, and in your food processor and pulse until powdery. Pour into a shallow bowl.
4. Pour the panko crumbs and parmesan cheese in another shallow bowl.
5. Roll the nuggets in the oatmeal mixture then the panko mixture.
6. Lay the nuggets on a foil lined baking sheet and lightly spray them with cooking spray.
7. Bake for 20 minutes, turning halfway through cooking time.

**Serve with green beans and Honey Glazed Carrots.

Lemon Pepper Chicken

Servings: 4-6

What you need:

1 tbsp olive oil

1 onion, chopped

3 tsp minced garlic

1 1/2 lbs chicken breasts

1 tbsp lemon pepper seasoning

1 tsp crushed red pepper flakes

Salt and pepper, to taste

1/2 cup chicken broth

What to do:

1. Chop your chicken into 1-inch pieces.
2. Heat the olive oil in a large skillet over medium-high heat.
3. Saute the onion and garlic fo r3 minutes.
4. Add the chicken to the pan and continue to cook for 7-10 minutes or until the chicken is cooked through. I always cut a couple bigger pieces of chicken so I can cut them in half to make sure they are completely cooked through at the end of cooking time.
5. Add the lemon pepper, red pepper, salt, and pepper and stir to combine.
6. Add the chicken broth and deglaze the pan and cook for another couple of minutes.

**Serve with pasta, rice, or quinoa.

Skillet Lasagna

Servings: 6

What you need:

1 lb ground beef

2 tsp Italian seasoning

1 tsp salt

1 tbsp minced garlic

1 package oven-ready lasagna noodles, broken into fourths

48 oz spaghetti sauce

1/2 cup chicken broth

1 cup ricotta cheese

1 cup shredded mozzarella cheese

What to do:

1. In a large pot, brown the ground beef then drain off the fat.
2. Season the browned ground beef with Italian seasoning, salt, and garlic.
3. Pour a third of the sauce on top of the meat, then add a layer of noodles. Repeat, ending with the sauce on top.
4. Evenly pour the chicken broth over everything in the pot.
5. Bring the pot to a boil and reduce heat to low and cook for 15 minutes. Stir gently every few minutes.
6. When the noodles are tender, gently stir in the cheeses.
7. Cover and let sit for five minutes then serve.

**Serve with Cheesy Garlic Bread.

Sweet and Spicy Salmon

Servings: 4

What you need:

1/4 cup honey

1 tbsp minced garlic

2 tbsp soy sauce

1 tbsp rice vinegar

1 tbsp sesame oil

1 tbsp grated ginger

2 tsp Sriracha

Pepper, to taste

2 lbs salmon

What to do:

1. Preheat your oven to 375 degrees F and line a baking sheet with foil.
2. In a small bowl, whisk together the honey, garlic, soy sauce, vinegar, oil, ginger, Sriracha, and pepper.
3. Place the salmon on the prepared baking sheet and fold the foil up around it.
4. Spoon the honey mixture over the salmon and fold the sides over it. Make sure the foil is sealed completely.
5. Place in the oven and bake for 15-20 minutes until the salmon is cooked through.
6. Open the foil and broil the salmon for 2 minutes.
7. Serve immediately.

**Serve with Roasted Asparagus or Sriracha Zucchini.

Broccoli Shrimp Stir Fry

Servings: 4

What you need:

1 tbsp olive oil
1 1/2 lbs shrimp, peeled and deveined
4 cups broccoli florets
1 tsp sesame seeds
3 tbsp soy sauce
1 tbsp rice vinegar
1 tbsp brown sugar
1 tbsp freshly grated ginger
2 cloves garlic
1 tsp sesame oil
1 tsp corn starch
1 tsp Sriracha

What to do:

1. In a small bowl whisk together the soy sauce, vinegar, brown sugar, ginger, garlic, oil, cornstarch, and Sriracha. Set aside.
2. Heat the olive oil in a large skillet over medium-high heat.
3. Once the skillet is hot, add in the shrimp and cook, stirring every few seconds, until they turn pink (about 2-3 minutes).
4. Add the broccoli to the skillet and cook, stirring every few seconds, for 3 minutes.
5. Stir the soy sauce mixture into the shrimp and broccoli and combine. Cook for 2 minutes or until the sauce is slightly thickened.
6. Serve immediately garnished with sesame seeds.

Garlic Butter Shrimp Pasta

Servings: 4

What you need:

8 oz fettucine noodles
1 lb shrimp, peeled and deveined
Salt and pepper, to taste
1 stick of butter, divided
4 tsp minced garlic
1/2 tsp dried oregano
1/2 tsp crushed red pepper flakes
2 cup baby spinach, roughly chopped
1/2 cup grated parmesan cheese

What to do:

1. Cook the pasta according to package directions and drain well.
2. Melt 2 tbsp of butter in a large skillet over medium high heat.
3. Add the garlic, oregano, and red pepper to the skillet and cook for 2 minutes, stirring frequently.
4. Add in the shrimp and cook, stirring frequently, for 2-3 minutes or until they are pink. Remove from skillet and set aside.
5. Melt the rest of the butter in the skillet and stir in the pasta, spinach, and parmesan cheese. Stir until the spinach begins to wilt, about 2 minutes.
6. Stir in the shrimp and serve immediately.

Pizza Pasta

Servings: 4-6

What you need:

8 oz penne pasta

1 package pepperonis

1 lb Italian sausage

1 small onion, diced

1 bell pepper, diced

1 tbsp minced garlic

1 tbsp Italian seasoning

1 16 oz jar pizza sauce

2 cups water

1 small can of tomato paste

2 cups beef broth

2 cups shredded mozzarella

What to do:

1. Heat the olive oil in a large skillet and sauté the onions and peppers for 5 minutes. Add in the garlic and sauté for 1 minute.
2. Add in the Italian sausage and pepperoni. Cook until the sausage is browned.
3. Stir in the pasta, beef broth, tomato paste, pizza sauce, water, and Italian seasoning. Bring to a boil then reduce heat to medium low.
4. Cover and simmer for 15 minutes or until the pasta is tender. Stir occasionally.
5. Remove from heat and stir in the cheese. Cover and let sit for a couple minutes to let the cheese melt then serve.

Creamy Chicken Spaghetti

Servings: 6-8

What you need:

1 package angel hair pasta

1 rotisserie chicken

2 cups shredded cheddar cheese

1 cup sour cream

1 can rotel tomatoes

1 can cream of mushroom soup

What to do:

1. Cook the angel hair pasta according to package directions and drain.
2. While the pasta is cooking, shred the rotisserie chicken.
3. In a large bowl, stir together the shredded chicken, sour cream, rotel tomatoes, and cream of mushroom soup.
4. After draining the pasta, stir the chicken mixture into the pot with the pasta.
5. Heat over medium-low heat for 5-10 minutes or until heated through.

Taco Soup

Servings: 8-10

What you need:

2 lbs ground beef
2 large cans tomato sauce
1 can white corn
1 can kidney beans
1 can rotel tomatoes
Salt and pepper, to taste
1 package taco seasoning

What to do:

1. Brown the ground beef in a large pot and drain.
2. Add in the rest of the ingredients and cook over medium heat for 15 minutes.
3. Serve with Fritos and cheese.

Sloppy Joes

Servings: 4

What you need:

1 lb ground beef

1 small can tomato sauce

1 tbsp Worcestershire sauce

1 tsp mustard

1 tsp salt

1 tsp pepper

1/2 tsp onion powder

1/2 tsp garlic powder

Hamburger buns

What to do:

1. Brown the ground beef in a large saucepan and drain well.
2. Add in the tomato sauce, Worcestershire, mustard, salt, pepper, onion powder, and garlic powder. Stir well and cook over medium-high heat for 5-10 minutes.
3. Serve on hamburger buns.

Shrimp and Grits

Servings: 6

What you need:

6 slices bacon, chopped
2 lb. (1 2 cups) shrimp (small to med.)
2 cups green onions, sliced
2 cups bell pepper, diced
2 cups mushrooms (optional), sliced
2 cups diced pimentos
1 tbsp parsley
1 tbsp lemon juice
2 tsp garlic powder
Salt and pepper, to taste
1 tbsp Worcestershire sauce
2 cups white wine (cooking wine works too)
Tabasco sauce, to taste
2 tbsp butter
Small can of tomato sauce
Grits

What to do:

1. Fry bacon pieces in a large skillet until just crisp, not hard. Remove to a bowl.
2. Drain all but 1 tbsp of the bacon fat from the skillet.
3. Add the shrimp to the skillet. Stir and cook for 2-3 minutes over medium heat. Remove shrimp and juices to bowl with bacon.
4. Add butter to the skillet. Sauté onions, pepper, and mushrooms until tender.
5. Add pimento, parsley, lemon juice, garlic, salt, Worcestershire, wine and Tabasco to the skillet.

6. When mixture comes to a simmer, add bacon and shrimp. Stir to mix all ingredients. Let simmer for 2-3 minutes.

7. Add small can of tomato sauce and simmer couple more minutes.

8. Cook 1/2 cup to 1 cup of grits per serving. Can add cheese if you like. Cook grits according to package directions.

9. Serve shrimp mixture over grits.

Salmon Patties

Servings: 4-6

What you need:
1 can Salmon, drained
1 egg
1 ½ cups cracker crumbs
Small diced onion or 1 tsp onion powder
1/2 tsp garlic powder
1 cup corn meal
1/2 cup flour
Cooking oil

What to do:
1. In a large bowl, mix together the Salmon, egg, cracker crumbs, onion, and garlic powder.
2. Form the mixture into small patties.
3. In a small bowl, mix together the corn meal and flour.
4. Roll the salmon patties in the corn meal mixture.
5. Fry in hot cooking oil until both sides are lightly browned.

**Serve with Mediterranean Vegetables.

Spaghetti

Servings: 4

What you need:

1 onion, chopped

1 tbsp olive oil

1 lb ground beef

28-oz can of crushed tomatoes

3 tsp minced garlic

1 tsp dried oregano

1 cup fresh chopped parsley

Salt and pepper, to taste

1/2 lb spaghetti noodles

Grated parmesan cheese, for serving

What to do:

1. Brown the ground beef in a large skillet over medium-high heat.
2. Drain and set aside.
3. Heat the oil in a large saucepan over medium-high heat and sauté the onion for 3 minutes.
4. Add water to a large pot. Salt the water and put it over medium-high heat. This is for boiling your noodles.
5. Add the garlic and sauté for 1 minute.
6. Add in the tomatoes, oregano, parsley, and the browned ground beef. Bring to a steady simmer.
7. Season with salt and pepper. Reduce heat to low and cook for 10 minutes.
8. Add the noodles to the water from step 4 when it starts boiling. Boil according to package directions.

9. Drain the noodles and serve topped with the meat sauce and parmesan cheese.

**While the sauce and noodles are cooking, prepare some cheesy garlic bread to go with the spaghetti!

Cheesy Garlic Bread

Servings: 4-6

What you need:

2 tsp minced garlic

1 large loaf of French bread

1 cup grated cheese

4 tbsp butter, at room temp

2 tbsp olive oil

1 tbsp dry Italian seasoning

What to do:

1. Heat your oven to 400 degrees F.
2. Cut loaf down the middle and place on a baking pan.
3. In a small bowl, mix together the butter, olive oil, garlic, and parsley.
4. Spread the butter mixture over the bread.
5. Top each side of the bread with cheese.
6. Bake for 5-8 minutes.
7. Remove from the oven and cut into strips.

Roasted Asparagus

Servings: 4

What you need:
1 bunch asparagus, ends trimmed
1 clove garlic, minced
2 tbsp olive oil
2 tbsp honey
1 tbsp balsamic vinegar
Salt, to taste

What to do:
1. Preheat your oven to 400 degrees F.
2. Mix the garlic, olive oil, honey, vinegar, and salt in a small bowl.
3. Place the asparagus on a lined baking sheet.
4. Pour the mixture evenly over the asparagus.
5. Roast for 15 minutes.

Sriracha Zucchini

Servings: 4

What you need:

1 lb zucchini, sliced

1 tbsp olive oil

1" piece of ginger, peeled and minced

3 cloves garlic, minced

2 tsp soy sauce

1 tsp sesame oil

2 tbsp Sriracha sauce

1/2 cup chopped cilantro

What to do:

1. Heat a large saucepan over medium heat and add the olive oil.
2. Stir in the ginger and the garlic and cook for 3-5 minutes.
3. Add the zucchini and cook for about 2 minutes.
4. Add the soy sauce, sesame oil, and Sriracha sauce. Stir well.
5. Cook for an additional 2 minutes.
6. Top with fresh cilantro before serving.

Honey Glazed Carrots

Servings: 4-6

What you need:

1 tbsp olive oil
2 lbs carrots, cut into 1-inch slices
1 cup chicken broth
1/2 cup honey
2 tbsp red-wine vinegar
Salt and pepper, to taste
2 tbsp butter

What to do:

1. Heat oil over medium-high heat in a large skillet.
2. Add the carrots and cook for about 2 minutes.
3. Add the broth, honey, vinegar, salt, and pepper to the skillet. Bring to a boil then reduce to a simmer. Cover and cook for 10 minutes.
4. Uncover and cook until carrots are tender and liquid has thickened, about 8-9 minutes.
5. Remove the skillet from the heat and add in butter and stir.

Mediterranean Vegetables

Servings: 4

What you need:

2 tbsp olive oil

2 medium zucchini

1 medium yellow onion, sliced

1 red bell pepper, sliced

2 tsp olive oil

2 tsp Greek seasoning

2 tsp balsamic vinegar

1/4 tsp garlic salt

1/4 tsp sugar

What to do:

1. Cut the zucchini into eighths lengthwise, then in half crosswise.
2. Add 2 tbsp of olive oil to a large skillet and heat over medium-high heat.
3. Add the zucchini, onion, and bell pepper to the skillet. Cook and stir for 6-8 minutes.
4. In a small bowl, whisk together 2 tsp olive oil, Greek seasoning, balsamic vinegar, garlic salt, and sugar.
5. Remove the skillet from the heat and drizzle on oil/seasoning mixture and toss well to coat.
6. Serve immediately.

30 Minute Meals

ABOUT THE AUTHOR

Hannie's vision is to write a series of recipe books, each focusing on one theme or one type of food that could can be EASILY prepared by someone who wouldn't be considered your typical cook. She urges her readers to feel welcome to share recipes, thoughts, and ideas with her and any feedback is encouraged.

For more recipe books visit hanniepscott.com

Made in the USA
Middletown, DE
20 October 2016